THE HITTING GAME

THE HITTING GAME
Graham Clifford

SEREN

Seren is the book imprint of
Poetry Wales Press Ltd.
57 Nolton Street, Bridgend, Wales, CF31 3AE
www.serenbooks.com
Twitter: @SerenBooks
facebook.com/SerenBooks

The right of Graham Clifford to be identified as
the author of this work has been asserted in accordance
with the Copyright, Designs and Patents Act, 1988.

ISBN: 978-1-78172-165-0
e-book: 978-1-78172-166-7
Kindle: 978-1-78172-167-4

A CIP record for this title is available from the British Library.

The publisher acknowledges the financial assistance of the Welsh Books Council.

Cover by:

Printed in Bembo by Bell & Bain Ltd, Glasgow

Author's Website: www.grahamclifford.co.uk

Contents

On the Dispersal of Water

It's 1:30 am.
He takes me away from the others unpacking,
opens the front door to the first night
in our first home and squirts WD-40
over both hinges, explains
WD is water dispersal,
NASA concocted this stuff
to keep fields of rockets
from turning orange, then burnt umber.

He heard this on his pocket radio
cycling along blustery city avenues
that curve between the reservoirs,
buffeted by daydreams of microwaves
and languorous AM waves,
walloped by the slipstreams of juggernauts
that don't recognise bike lanes
on B roads where streetlights refuse to work.

He holds up my key and lubricates it
with a quick squirt of the clear oil,
slips it still wet in the lock
to revitalise inner gubbins:
he knows all the proper names.
When I turn my back to go inside
this kind man takes the squeak from the gate.

Swallows

These birds, each only a slim book's weight,
are strong, years old
and flick about dusk like black flames.

They have shoulders and attitude.
Tensing their sector of umbrella
jerks them across the path,
passing my face so close
I feel the chill from air sliced.
They seem to want to cut me up.

It is as if they're bitter
and are demonstrating the impatience of fathers
sick of working smoking bitumen
into holes in roofs or tar into roads.

I'm doing nothing to them
but it's as if my leisure looks like disrespect
and I am, therefore,
asking for it.

Towards Morning

I'm searching for sleep, for its AM frequency.
I wind down, thumbing focus onto
purple throbs, over a serious clicking –
it's that satellite in a deteriorating orbit.

I carry on through the numbers, find
an analogue sitcom in Urdu
recorded under a duvet
then a Dalek commentating on hurling
from inside a baked bean can, then
there's a channel dealing in clean-cut chat,
talk in a forever rising tone that suggests
an answer just around the corner, or, if not,
then definitely round the next.

A fifties heat ray wipes everything out
except machinery
by some fluke transmitting its own *chug,*
                                        chug
and I'm one foot in the Land of Nod
until the fast, crunchy beat of a speeding heart
that bleeds ever outwards. I move on,

get the end of a theme tune
always humming at the centre of me, then arrive
at the proper AM doldrums:
an outdoor conference in the rain in Paris,
Alpha 60 broadcasting to *The Lands Without,*
a brass band on its own in a barn, poised,
world-shattering formulae hastily chalked up,
glass rims keening, congress erupting a corridor away,
a Theremin concert audience in corduroy
being seated without word or cough,
real Morse code, trains, rain tutting on a tent,
a stylus shushing when the last
of the spiral becomes a circle in vinyl.

In Love with Mr Jiggs

This man loves his chimp,
though she's a female
I call her Mister Jiggs.
Soaping her belly in widening circles,
some might wonder how clean he makes her.
With auburn hair, grey roots, tight skin,
in a life made of days off,
walking Mister Jiggs to the stores she can't go in,
picking Mister Jiggs up when she falls
from her scooter, or red skateboard.

Mister Jiggs kisses his elbow
when he slaps her solid brow,
You old coconut head! Everyone knows
he's the boy punching a girl he likes best.
Mister Jiggs loves her programmes.
Mister Jiggs wears a nappy, just in case.
Last year she was fifty.
She laps her soup when he isn't looking,
spoons shakily when he is.

She sleeps all night now
under a duvet printed with jungle animals.
He tucks her in and turns off the telly,
pushes her head too hard into the pillow,
draws the curtains, but it's early
and light for hours yet.

Song for Empty Rooms

Everyone came in at different times:
the boy with no friends who sang so well
that everybody noticed and he sunk it,
irretrievably.

A fat girl who mumbled the daft lyrics into her chest
while two spiteful bitches spat at her back
and the hated song went on about love

and the well-shaped girls at the front sang too high
to hide, and the boy mostly asleep standing up realised
in the rafters is a boat

and the girl with a moustache sang deep as a man
while the boy with no dad laughed
and laughed at the boy with two mums who sang
like bubbles struggling through mud
and got told off for it, made to sing on his own
and did, in tears, until they realised it was him
so told everybody *Enjoy it!*
Feel it! Move us!

and the boy with the most friends felt utterly alone
while outside, the music of afternoons
wasted itself:
drilling, the sore buzz
of tiles being cut overlaid on a siren
at the edge of hearing,
the hammering of men that always sat at the back
who'd spent their days fingering cracks
and curls of prehistoric Sellotape, touching splinters
on the flipside of where sums got done.

Men carrying with them
the feeling of being perpetually in the wrong place,
except when standing in empty rooms
with windows without glass.

Milt

It's snowing, and settling
and he is remembering what he wore
and the names of cab drivers and travellers

when he tells you how he slid
down the world's pocked cheek
into a trampled paradise.

How the heat pushed into him
and when the boss-sun backed off
the heat would rise out of everything but him

so even in midnight winds
on a rented speedboat's integral diving board
he was hot, his every atom altered for good.

Here is the lucky photo someone took
of him walking on water
a moment before he was under his element

where the splurge of electric light
caused once-in-a-lifetime anemones
to part, absent-mindedly, with clouds of milt.

Santa and Sand Flea

Sunburnt in September on flat roofs
nearer the daytime, Paracetamol moon,
what a colour his skin went:
of corrosion and honey,
top layers caramelised.

There is a photo
of him hand-standing, wrists thick
as my ankles, skin a tight suit,
gas-bottle tense, broom-fit
but he rolled up under us
close to the sofa on Sundays, taking cover
from the jagged migraine of Mondays.

Perpetually on edges,
Army Surplus steel toecaps squeezing
the sweat from moss, working
at the trembling frontier of out-of-reach.
There was a weir and millpond I never saw
tickled by nettles and pussy willow,
where dragonflies with gold-sieve eyes
bit into skiving men made mostly of sausage,
and his eyes were the blue
of Light Ale can lettering
or too-clever collies' eyes.

Life got in through cracks he made:
a woman's name that wasn't mum's for our Granada
when the engine blackened and spat
on an incline into the holidays.

PhD in ladders, thief, dictator,
Santa and sand flea,
he hopped across rock pools,
smashed to bits a crab that got me
then swung himself into a shipwreck –

from the sideways door, he made it perfectly clear
how stupid it would be to even try to follow.

No Alternative Now

Let's grow a forest and hide in it.
We will stay there for years,
our clothes dropping from us in leaf shapes
in the dim crunchiness
where we copulate quickly like foxes,
and crap standing, ready to run.

After a while, reporters will arrive
but we will be up a tree,
bearded and matted.

Puffballs come up in the areas where we urinate:
they are delicately luminescent,
buzz in the dark like candlelit, drizzly planets.

Shivering, curled together, one night
I smell death about to bloom in you –
next thing, you don't want your hazel nuts,
can't pull yourself up onto our branch.

From then on, until it happens,
every night I dream we drive sharp cars
and eat from tins.
We will never get this life out of our system.

Trying

You tell me there wasn't one midwife
but you were visited by a set of four
on a rotating shift and when you split
like an overripe *momento mori* fig
it happened to be the nice one
with different David-Bowie eyes,
who stank of smoke,
telling you to breathe – like you'd forget!

You shift up closer
and, staring, ask about our trying
then tickle my knee to describe how it will first feel:
some blind fluttering, like a moth
that wastes its powder inside cupped hands.

Stealing Summer

He sprawls among pregnant old men
bewildered in baseball caps,
and bristled, pork-crackling wives.

Worn-out evergreens flop and nod
insects into the quivering, cyan pool.

His wife swats a butterfly off her belly,
Velcros on a tin-foil collar
to encourage sunlight up her nose.

The abnormally affectionate, hotel moggy pads over
dozy from being black in the sun
to show off a blood-flecked starfish.

It's always summer here.
Or at least late spring.
Daydreaming at a gull
his gaze smudges the chalk-dust moon.

Orchids blurt livid smears.
A tights-coloured jelly-fish flops and folds over
and inside-out in a meek tide
that dabs the beach
like it's at work and being watched.

He barely sleeps all week,
garlic soup and frappé fermenting
along sore, demijohn innards.

But when his eyelids do slide closed,
his Lilo chafing the pool side's concrete lip, or
wound in his sheets, a bleached dawn
too soon seeping from the blinds,
he dreams a muffling inch of snow has settled
on date palms and hire cars.

Child Development

I am concerned we are making this mother
not like her son
by bringing to the surface in a rush
all his faults
to find out why he won't sit still
and does what he does.

He looks fatter recently,
and turns his toes inwards
in a way that I've always liked but know
is aberrant, or will lead to aberrations.

And he looks over his shoulder often.
We have talked of how
he will escape
to the safe middle-distance
where ground-down words become music,

and how he will look for your eyes.
We have been told
we should not hold his gaze
in case he gets in and draws from us
what he thinks he needs,
what we are advised isn't helping.

I saw the thinnest slice of a moon this morning.
Tomorrow, it will be melted and gone.

What I Wrote

Do you remember what I wrote
on the back of my German book,
about Miss Moore, as some sort of joke,
and how she sent me to Fossey?
He had old, elephant ears
and a tin in his heart.

When I proffered *das Buch*
he churched his fingers
and told me to read what I'd written
then read it again, but this time
slow,
so the words could hurt us both properly.

I read and he leaned back
away from me.

The Hitting Game

On the island's south side
a solitary town fizzes
like overloaded circuitry
on dark, motherboard hills.

Across a sticky, smooth-tiled walkway
an amusement arcade spills
a test of sexiness based on how moist your palm is
and the hitting game.

You spin in coins so they register
on sensors worn numb.
A padded stump protuberates.
The screen says HIT IT! A bell rings
but everyone's watching
and your hasty jab glances off
compacted plastic quilting. Missing
makes you totter. It's your second go,

the screen says HIT IT! The bell rings.
A slurp of adrenalin lop-sides your heart
and this time, when
your half-arsed haymaker connects,
an industrial spring kicks back,
jolts your arm.
Sweat prickles through burnt skin

it's your third and last chance
to prove yourself
and the screen says HIT IT! so you hiss
come on you fucking fucker, fuck you.

The bell rings, you duck down half an inch
to push against the planet, bite the air
even if you're the type to walk in the shade,

even if you've learnt to not want
and know when to stop,
even if you've never, ever, your whole life,
intentionally hurt anyone
but yourself.

Newborn

She nearly isn't here. So soft
I have to watch to know
I've touched this pink steam
somehow holding her shape.

Dimmer switch screwed almost shut
we are stock-still
nocturnal desert-mammals, saucer-eyed,
cramping in thunder-struck poses.
Her spider-leg eyelashes
rest on a web that has us while she dreams
the leaf-edge of her country.

Unfurling by millimetres in spiked air,
anemone fingers splay then clench
as she tunes herself in,
becomes herself minutely, frost
fringing the shore of the cleanest puddle.

How to Hurt

John slumped in the shower
in the submarine
and died six weeks later.

He could sound like Donald Duck
and speak Russian
but we weren't supposed to know.
My copy of Tom Waits' *Blue Valentine*
and *The Diamond as Big as the Ritz*
by F. Scott Fitzgerald were his.
He had a long grey raincoat
and was twenty-six.

While everyone busied themselves
I was sent to stay with Nan and Granddad
who didn't like me watching the A-team
because it was *terribly violent*
although they had been in the war.

Rosy with morning sherry
Granddad slopped proper fat on my toes.
Skin bubbled
and at the edge of the pitch
my best friend trod exactly on them
with studs, so don't think
I was too young then for real pain.

Indispensable

Our heads subtly tilt when we read
all the small print
on leaflets from banks
and manuals for appliances.

We have never
accidentally paid too much
and have so many close friends,
each enjoying an equal share of our love.

We choose to holiday
in countries always brisk with wind,
to picnic among sharp, dune grasses
watching waves curl on beaches
that begin and end out of sight.

We eat to live.
Our children are fat, their features
sunk like stones slung in mud.
Soon, their overnight transformation
into aloof, direct adolescents
will make us shine from the inside.

We choose when. And where.
We carefully flick the crumbs
from rubbings out.

Your parents were intelligent;
years before, deposited their feelings
inside a terrier that died.

Mine jog the park perimeter and shortcuts
where cubes of windscreen glass
crunch underfoot, they confess
to a quickening of the pulse
walking alleys tense with the flutter
of breaking-down streetlight.

We do not believe in getting old.
Our talent is indispensable
in your messy, storming world.

What I Really Want to Do

In the hotel I wait in a fresh suit,
the material hanging on me cold and heavy.
My palms are clammy, cheeks burn
from adrenalin or thinking. Muffled TV applause
and premiership results haunt the air.
I'm about to piss again when he arrives,
shakes my hand well then leads me
by the grinning receptionist, down thin stairs
past a heated, kitchen tête-à-tête in Twi,
into a back room.

Through the net curtain there is a wall.
A two bar electric heater
from a Giles cartoon has filched the oxygen.
He asks me to sit. I already have
so he thanks me for coming and
thanks me for wearing a suit and I say
it's new, this morning, I'm trying it out
to see if it works and he laughs.

He asks the big one first,
What do I want to do? But he's friendly
and funny and he wants me to be frank
so I tell him, I'm lost, unsure
and he tells me my CV is intriguing, a jigsaw
with bits missing then extra bits,
snippets from another scene. And that's funny.
But what do I want to do?

He tells me about him: he loves opera.
His hands are thick and small and he's perspiring
in the receding Vs and he writes
articles on interview techniques for IT graduates,
and reviews opera.

He doesn't say for whom.
Sometimes he's in Geneva.
He has a suit on. No tie: it is Saturday.
But what do I really want to do?

I hold my hands out, palms up.
They're empty.

Silage

That winter, clammy under smothering togs
anticipating balls poised inside
like nukes in a bomb bay, to drop...
I was a hot spot.

And every Hercules
rehearsing down the flight-path hypotenuse
just feet above my chip-board cabin-bed,
the aerial a counter needle wagging
atomizing hope of vertical hold,
was Cruise.

Sleep, slick as silk sheets, slid off.
Churning, low cloud murmured
with Tartrazine landing-light
and revving engines reflected
over a bull-dozer-ed dyke,
scooped and shoved in order to hide

tail fins that milled like a tank of starved sharks.
Horny, they'd taxi to the runway edge
then swing round, writing knots with wheel rubber
and just miss tangling propellers,
discs of razor fog. Aching to go,
they never went.

A Man Who Had Formed His Adult Self According to Questionable Parameters, Initiates Change

The recorded guide tells me
this bituminous triptych
was for aiming private devotions
at the three scrawny martyrs
each posed with a symbol
of their bespoke torture:
a wheel, a key, a beard.

I order them prettiest first
then message a God-shaped space
to make these girls, heads bowed
as if it was their fault,
more important to me
than my own reflection in the glass.

No response.
Each minute of every day
is catalogued in the hard drive of me
and the adamantine future
will not be cracked, so

I force myself to imagine I love
the bearded saint:
I kiss her beard and raise
hirsute daughters with her in the past.

Then I imagine my friends there.
And the noise they make
when they find out.
How that does not stop.

Skinned

The lad in the cafe at the end of the pier
is so wrecked by puberty we're afraid he might forget
to breathe. He's a skinned nerve,
a child in a man-suit fumbling our tea and biscuits.
I pay with pocket-warm coins and our fingers touch.
He flicks a glance at me with eyes like bullet holes.

Poor sod. I remember the throb
in my leg bones in dinner queues at school;
how, elongating on the sofa I begged
mum to knead my calves; how
one muggy evening, a bloke stared back from the
                                        wardrobe mirror
daring me with a frown to solve

the numbing blush, to explain
why his best friend was no longer anywhere near enough.

On Being Temporary

On the first day of summer proper
I upturn my wrists,
pale as undersides of shy snakes,
to cold water.

The chill of subterranean pipes
presents metal to the heart,
a memory of winter
to be slingshot throughout
the road map of arteries veins capillaries,
a leafless tree branching
in textbook surgical-purple and crimson.

Cooler. Cooler still. Cool –
I shrink in the room
or the walls back away,
sweat recedes down pores
as the last drop backs up
into the tap wound tightly closed.

I am refocused to fit inside myself.
Exact, tight-edged,
I step back into the overheated world
and this charm is gone.

Bitumen and Rust

In the end you didn't buy an angle-poise light
called *Lack* – it must mean something aspirational
in another language. Driving home, a green-brass prick

of a church wedged in-between semis began to glow
as if a prayer just got answered. As if. Polystyrene
tea in cup holders. Dirty little seas rich as slicks

of sewage-juice in ruts we trudged in a landscape
ruined with bitumen and rust, by slung piglet carcasses
still eyeing fly-tipped, shoddy white goods.

There is more than one disputed memory
we tug apart like foxes: under branches
sweating out winter, the colder, wet side of freezing

I found clay pigeon shrapnel like smashed, thick 45s.
You first saw the sun drown in two ponds at the outskirts
where *where we know* turned into *where we don't.*

Spuds and beet surfaced from dirt, sick bits;
it was me that bit an onion like an apple. Barbed wire –
you slam on the brake so as not to kill

a man selling premature roses in the road.
Everyone is full of music to make it better.
Jittery clouds scarper to the margin like bath foam,

soap-touched. Suddenly, above us is baby blue.
You won't be around forever; laugh: tea –
barbed wire that disappeared into tree bark.

Anger

This anger is pointless
as Tiger's eye storms
unseen at sea,
rain pitting the waves
with fitful number.

While you clench
around such violence,
talking and staying
are victories.

You can even smile,
say you're fine
as breakers swell to smash
rudimentary dwellings.

A momentary shudder:
sea-spray sculptures
of yourself
reach in agony,
burst into mist.

Bookshelves

I'm approximately nowhere
lying sideways on weddings, wondering
what narcissism means to me.

An old Sharon sweeps the room
of blood, tin and straw
weighed down by her own clever daughter,
lightning picnics and the earliest
of English poems.

There is a Dutch vigil in a triggering town.
The Rampage effects
what work was. Blood
on the axe, bursting clouds on the contrary,
labyrinths of essays, the world's wife
reads the sea to the west.
I knew all this.

The Dwarf; The Factory; The Aftermath.
In that order.

Billy the Kid, making certain it goes on,
gets so alone.
Such frost.
Luck.

Sick flowers in flames cause
much writing home, I suppose.
It takes more than you have
to wring a tear out of me.

At this point, I will only settle for
any short sentence of my own.

The History of Patches

He enters the cupboard
under the sink,
contorting past the gas meter
that doles out therms
with one whistling, blue exhale
blown through spendthrift gas rings.

He has a fresh rubber hose
moist as cheese
pure enough to teethe on,
its smoky, scrapyard stink
ekes into my hands and lips
when I play it like a trunk
pea-shooting a monkey nut,
cracking one on the lunar Artex.

The kitchen opens itself up:
a history of patches toasted
with tea after tea after tea.

Lines of Desire

We should have known it was a mistake
to revisit the locally famous beauty spot
which did the job, only yesterday.

The weather was the same, if not better.
The light, again, brought back those smeary,
off-set re-productions of Hitchens and Sisley.

The gravel seemed so looked at. Leaves too,
with photons and oxygen pouring out and through.
But we were un-tuned, now bored on desire lines

by rudely healthy nettles and blackberry pickups;
a crisp packet in the same spot; your aura so ragged
and at odds, puncturing mine. I'm sick of this

trampling of scenes for how they soothed us,
only yesterday. Gone today. Tonight, blood-shot,
we can only squint into ordnance survey maps; pack

then carefully repack the cool box; imagine
what it could be we need to see next that will make it
ever so briefly all right being us.

Amazing

the talk you talk for hours
as if each word is white hot
to be gobbed out before it burns.
You leap days
and continents like a superhero
so much to tell, so little time and you're right:
the mitten-ed arson threatens it,
worn out broilers at work, those ants,
the first twinge of a toenail growing down.

Inhale: then your Dad cuts in,
his ox tongue can't/won't lay still
so it's science and BT cables,
the piggyback of info down ISDN lines
(I still don't get it)
the long weight of the moon, bread crumb stars
and his misplaced brother, sewn up
with fluff behind a jacket's lining.

Another re-spray, tread worn bald,
the price of tea till our innards are tanned
when your Mum storms in with a thirst for cheese
and it's Alf about to shake himself to bits,
the letter he wrote, pen in both hands, to thank her.

And the headlines, yesterday's
from three doppelganger tabloids,
the ins and outs of tragedy as seen from
the dark side of a dining table
and it's the fires still belching and a stupid war
raging stupidly that briefly winds us.

Under What We Live On

These hills are riddled with tunnels and ducts and pipes.
Wiring on its way nowhere sprouts
like numbered liquorice among snowdrops.
Brick work has caved in leaving
a ruined mouth in the grass.
Trimmed Bakelite switches turn up in molehills
in a field with no gate. An urgent, square copse
has grown through the pylon on its side,
lifting it up, swaying it
an inch above humus and clay pigeon shrapnel.
Thin moss clings to an airfield you won't find on maps.
Metal detectors whine like the last whale.
This has everything to do with what doesn't get taught,
what you have to make up for yourself.

Running-up

It's hot.
Bitter-shandy slops cook
in tea-tray dents, boozy wasps
tip-toe through sweet froth.
Gravel chips flicked-up off soft roads
set like dumb gems in loaves of road paint,
chewy as raw gold.
The sky is grubby as B&B pillows.
Any dreams are of billowing, nautical skies
when the first swifts scythed back
shaving tarmac with screeching arcs.
Living is a chore today.

A bloated jumbo jet wants out
of the upturned pudding bowl
of cloud cover. It sneaks along
like a failing spider on a ceiling.
Sparrows pant through chipped beaks.
A bridge's pipe-work reflection
wobbles on the grease-canal.
I push on glasses, hang my head,

pea-green smoke wavers inches below.
A billion ingenious pips are chugging
against a sloppy current.
Like astigmatic irises jigging to compensate,
daphnia are swarming
doing better than okay in tasty muck,
going somewhere and finding an ending.
In the heavy-metal-rich gloom
they're multiplying, dancing, evolving:
winning.

Minor Poet for the 21st Century

This book has been checked out
three times in a decade,
Minor Poets of the 18th Century.
It is wrapped in a rifle-green
sticky, dust jacket.

I open it, strum pages to release
that delicious, decomposing-wood perfume
second-hand book sellers wear.

Long, miniscule bugs retreat to the spine
with a sense of me,
something too big to focus on.

This book is a foolscap gravestone,
a memorial for the most capable also-rans,
what they used their best hours up on
and succeeded in getting
perfectly not-quite-right,

navigating dust maelstroms
in the airless fug of thought-crammed studies,
on their shelves, perhaps, a mint copy

Minor Poets of the 15th Century.

Drawing Circles

I shall draw
one faultless freehand circle.

Gradual, meticulous
further than naturally capable,
I dredge exactitude
rotating the page,
feathering my way around.

This is not what I want you to see:
me, tense. Pained.

Others try, with wrist flicks.
Some almost do it!
They dab, swirl, fail,
fall back into cushions
to cooing, while I

erase hours of grey travel
to begin again
getting it wrong again.

(In the end I get it right).

About my Daughter

How right the word seems,
so drawn out,
the *er?*-ing sound of *doubt*
abutting *ought.*

I stand in the dark
taking heat from you
spasming to slip my grip
full of voodoo, my daughter
a little scarecrow stuffed with eels
curling and flipping to get away.

Used light from cars
queasily slides across the wall,
shards and slices identically rearrange
with such recurring precision –
this long trapezoid, that misty rhombus
locked into the same move as tomorrow,
then its tomorrow.
A deadlocked endgame.

Doubt; ought; her. Daughter.
At last loose in my arms,
I lay you as if broken
into sleep's black mouth.

Talking about Gravity with Great Danes

Across the park's sunken plateau
an Italian greyhound pings:
a cocky whip of hazel,
bird's weight, nothing but a mote
sliding down her oily eye.

Half dust, half balding tractor-tyre,
half front-room diplodocus
pulling herself through air
as if fathoms under,
she is retreating, desiccating at extremities:
a bloody frosting where nose becomes fur,
claws worn to the nerve and vein.

A bark escapes her valley-chest,
a night shout
from inside a wood behind a hill.

Her skeleton rubs to get out,
creaks like a new boat.
A barrel-ribcage clicks at every exhale,
has an invisible circus hundredweight bearing down.
Days are sucked through a tight straw.

When she runs
a Dutch barge turns into waves
begins circling the globe the wrong way.
A stone table gallops. Giraffes are spooked.

You can see,
where red lids flop away, a neighbour
who was old when you were young
growing again, wordless, inside.

The Dust That Cuts

Over your shoulder the landscape flattens,
pillboxes tip backwards into the mud,
planted and ploughed around.
One has a sudden tree inside, deformed,
filling the low, concrete room
with stifled hope, pouring leaves
out to a negligent sun.
Kids bend in, draw up their knees
and stare-out days.

A half-kilometre of decrepit warehouses
signalling a town
were very graffitied, a decade ago.
Repeatedly, one word.
On crumbling floors, anxiously-frisky pigeons
fan-up dust that cuts.

Next is houses
that join so well to fields
combine harvesters and pronged machinery
scrape brickwork, crowd small windows,
move war shadows over display crockery.

There is a prized local sausage
chequered with blue-white fat.
An underground lake
like a buried, liquid moon. Then
this factory that slow-breathes those who stayed:

from the canteen they can see
turbine blades slicing over kempt hills.
With dolour they wind each weekend in.

Metamorphoses

You tell our daughter
that by this time next year
she will grow another foot.

She looks down, says
she'd rather a cat's tail
and bulls' horns on me
coursing with blood like a frog's
that can freeze.

And she wants you with
heron wings so huge
that when they're flapped
ornaments we never meant to accumulate
on a mantel piece we didn't plan,
would leap and shatter.

On dehumidified air curls a phrase
of a song from years ago, one of those
I can't choose to listen to
because of the direct tunnel it opens
to something we aren't any more –
just for now.

We part to different rooms
and wait
for a lamb's shoulder to cease bleeding.

How the sweet fat changes everything.

Protection

You would first say, *Oh!*
as if a shopping bag had split, except
it will be that a life has dropped out
with such simplicity

what we made on our own
unplugged, recalled
without ceremony or permission.
Gone. Like yesterday.

But I am becoming prepared.
Inured, like a zoo primate considering faces.
I'm disappearing hurt,
prematurely widening hairline fractures –

due to gape and reveal me, anyway –
so all that heat can rise out.
If I can think it first, perhaps
I will be protected.

Ancestors curled inside genes
dangle one-way instructions
for how to get by: lower your eyes; be patient;
attend to the littlest things.

Proof

You were right! All summer the flour
sweating in plastic quarantine;
sealed, clement-weather activated mites.
Tens of thousands behind thousands,
the grains have been switched
for pinpricks of existence, proof for your fears.
They are performing a sickening dance,
a familiar, mobilising shiver, devouring focus,
a synchronised crawl away from
what? Towards where?

Reaching past oblivious for
tins of tuna or a wine glass, or out
meeting friends in the park
a double-decker jet cuts a sudden
caesura through conversation,
bluntly threads clouds with exhaust noise
while, in our musty, fecund cupboard
just one of your worries
birthed a million eager facts.

Returning

through blue, putrid geography.
Coppices hunch on the ridge.
Forgotten wells overspill.

Between leftovers of forest
a stag leads hinds diagonally.
It looks back, counting.

Wood rains up as grey spores.
Farm scrap un-tenses into rust:
here is a dementia of things.

One hoof in a ditch. Bridges sag.
The sky bulges-down with the weight
of water. Almost touches.

A view of the Downs defers to memory:
cornfields mottled with airship shadows.
Roots throttle defunct mechanics.

Fog in cones under streetlights
swarms like brook daphnia.
Thermals bloat over dark meadows.

Houses approach; come together; back off.
Knotgrass scissored to reveal the path
is fur shaved for a cut.

In Cars

In cars, I'm him.
I make the shapes he makes.
One-hand-ing the steering wheel
as if gripping mane,
I cup the gear stick bulb
like it's a brandy bowl
and coast to junctions
clutch disengaged
because of what happens to sharks
should they stop

though on open road
I'll box in better cars than mine.
A sudden stickler for the limit
I slap and squeeze your knee
celebrating damming flow,
carbon monoxide whistling
from a leaf-choked vent.

What damage we do in cars.
I twist in my seat
then back up, bump bumpers,
wrench the handbrake;
it will take both your hands to undo.

That look in the mirror is all about me.
My shirt sticks.
In cars I'm him: you drive.

Restoring "graham"

... in the event of failure
or malfunction...
Collins English Dictionary

Should everything go wrong
all will revert to factory settings:

a couple of hundred high frequency words
in a West Country accent;
the smell of Talcum, and jumper wool
after a Sunday morning roasting pork;
shoulder-length hair, lighter from the sun;
flared second-hand 501s brimmed over;
the recurring dream of being able to back flip;
your hand making the Millennium Falcon
skimming hedges; TV warming up
in the next room; cloud-rammed evenings;
a long, plummeting cello chord
from the music on a cigar advert;
perpetual municipal shrubbery;
the phone ringing – it's always for you;
freckles they say will fade but don't
until you decide you want them
charting teeming constellations
even on your lips.

This program is installed as a failsafe.
Good luck.

The Best Poem Ever Written

I write a poem that is the best. Massive.
Not just long, but huge intellectually
and although it is book-length
reading is like freefalling,
each line greased with two genius thoughts.

The poem makes me famous.
I wander oxygen-depleted nights
down city streets and hear
lines of my poem bartered
between moist lovers.

On the train, I peek over the top
of a hardback book about me
at a man in a suit nodding off
and recognise the words he's mouthing in his swoon.

All front pages, every day,
showcase stanzas of my poem –
bombings and murders get tucked inside.
The new novelist pays well
to get my poem printed as an introduction:
she knows her work makes no sense without it.

Everyone I have ever known
rings me to ask how I did it.
I say I don't know, and that's the truth.
After a year the fuss hasn't died away.

I sit at my computer
and hear next door turn the TV on.
I put my ear to the wall.
It's an actor and he's reading my poem.
It's a good version: I've heard it before.

He has a Shakespearean voice
doing justice to what the introducer called
The Best Poem Ever Written.
I listen to it all, I travel where the poem takes me
then get back in my chair
and write a better one.

No-one, Son of Nobody

The great man Aesop saw his master pissing as he walked.
'What!' he exclaimed, 'ought we then to shit as we run?'
        – Michel de Montaigne, *Essays*.

To be a no-one, son of a nobody
from a centuries-long league of slowcoaches
and do-nothings, what a result! To be able
to run a finger up any fork in the family tree,
either side, and find, guaranteed every time,
semi-professional cloud gazers,
whittlers and amblers, time-wasters
dawdling the scenic route back,
plump folk who had the guts
and compassion to decline
every chance to convert promise.

It's easy, getting on: before you know it
CVs concertina-out, something mumbled
behind a hand in a corridor
winds up drastically pertinent. Right place,

right time. You get linked, tagged,
locally known, then internationally,
till you don't want to go out.
       Your friends,
the ones you are sure were stupid, now
it's them fowling the world's pretty cheek.
They own children of vicious intelligence.

They injection-mould plastic fins and paddles,
unnecessary sharpnesses.

I consider what you would say
if you thought I was even imagining
saying no to it all:
                    loyalty cards,
the latest thing in mauve;
Dolce & Gabbana suitcases, garden heaters; a rise
then a rise then a rise. Then a rise.

Sex and Death

When we first met
I want anything you have, you said
so we are lucky.

Desperate to find the missing parts of ourselves
we tried new things
like falling asleep me in you.

You were twenty and one day
washed the mascara off
but I couldn't see why your eyes were so different.
I stared and wouldn't let you turn away
the morning before I drove back
with a sore midriff
for Granddad's funeral.

There were no speeches
but your smell on my fingers
and *The Dambusters* theme tune.

Someone should have said
something.

B Movie

In a week it went from dry speck
to plump currant
so they cut it out
but threw him away,
bundled him into the incinerator
with mucked sheets
and sticky scalpel blades.
Chimneys piped blue smoke
into slow-churning clouds

and now it's big, sitting in his chair
watching the match on his television.
Though it can't see, it squints
where an eye would be
and says if it faces to the side
it can make out a ball,
the dresser leaving a leg out,
pound coins in a mess of change....

It is breathing, but
as if through a wet flannel,
and it's getting redder. And bigger.

Although there's no mouth with which to eat,
and nothing left to say, it tells me
to pass on its love to everyone, but to
keep a bit of that love for myself.
That's how I know.

The Oxygen Thieves

When she teaches about tenths
or silt in the slow-bending Severn
it is to the space above each
as if the adults they will be are there,
grown up phantoms
stood behind their earlier selves
and she can see the future ghosts
so addresses them
not the oxygen thieves
yawning like cats in front of her.

She tells me that sometimes they come back.
She laughs and says how, usually
the very worst slope in vapid
with the fatigue of work, or of no work,
and apologise, eyebrows high, and promise
that if they ever get anything
they'll leave it to her in their will
and if they could only have it all over
they would – they swear on their lives – sit still.

Shorn

Despite photos, up close
you are not taking care of yourself:
hair greasy as barbed-wire wool.

Your once skinny frame
is bulky at the shoulders' end
and lugworm veins bulge
on the backs of your hands.
What a thud you would make,
falling down now.

I feed the Wahl trimmer, mow
a broadening wicket
till you are Presley enlisted, or Travis Bickle
about to always be lucky with mistakes.
Your ear is rigid with sarsaparilla –
does this one hot and red mean something good?

We come across all the grey, dumbstruck as Eloi.
I steady myself on your cold, man's shoulder
to trim straight.

You say good weather only ever reminds you
of previous good weather
so I am sheering you of the past,
catching it on today's newspaper
and you are morphing: victim; perpetrator.

Finally, you pose and flex in the mirror
as if entering the city for the first time:
lighter; streamlined. Shorn.
Yet another you
only, this time

Obvious Constellations

I decide to be better than you.
It doesn't take long because you aren't much good:
you don't seem to care.

I become a sweeter talker,
more words per minute, a greater variety.
They come out naturally longer, now.

And I'm a superior walker, i.e. I never don't have
some part of either foot in contact with the tarmac
at any one time. I am covered

with more follicles per square centimetre. My job
pays significantly more per hour (I don't think about it).
You don't care my wife is fuller than yours;

my one son, more focused than your two
vague daughters – when did you last see them?
Look at my calf muscles; the contents of shopping basket;

your face in my alloys: you don't care.
I sit outside my bigger house and know
the majority of more obvious constellations,

the Latin name for a moose, how valves really are
and what transistors do. You sleep soundly; OK.
But I know why.

The Door

The door doesn't feel like it fits
when you close it, open it
to re-close it. Then again. And again.

Despite all that money
it will not shut properly.
A vacuum is compromised, or
an infinitesimal imperfection has fruited
its weakness, and now
the door will not close as it did
just an hour ago, when the outside
was stepped out of, locked apart,
left to its screensaver work
of passing traffic and blue tits.

This door was supposed to see you out.
You were not expecting
to have to re-consider
the fickle prettiness of versions;
what lethargy such decisions inspire.

I agree when I try: something is amiss,
then I fill with familiar guilt
because of our past
which swings beneath us like rotting udders
producing rotten milk.

A Train on the Street, October 22, 1895

Photograph by Kuhn

A locomotive
has devastated the Gare de L'Ouest.
It overshot the platform
and now balances on its front,
the coal truck and first passenger carriage
resting precariously behind.
A black iron zigzag.
Passers-by buzzed about too quick
to fix on the negative.

Industry and history and iron
has added up wrong.
This is a vision
plus muscle versus loiterers,
the not-to-be-trusted.
This is a Coke can
rolled under a brake pedal
as the lights go red, and
this is all crowds that congregate
at scenes of uncovering
who know there is beauty here –

here, where you embrace
every mistake
and know how, surely, your own heart
will one day burst from the front
you take to work each morning,
to present itself lumpen,
screaming its steam into
empty, indifferent streets.

Tempus Fugit

I know you best
as a list of sayings:
legends on key fobs,
bumper sticker one-liners,
wisdom broadcasting from
t-shirts, and this

antique damage
that travels through us,
now exiting like a stepped-on needle
which emerges, years later, rusted
from under the opposite ankle.

This pebble of saying
that once made a neat,
almost imperceptible entrance
now ripples countries-wide,
tsunamis-high.

Hearing it, we leave
and stay simultaneously:
watching the quilt-work history of fields
drop away; squinting to see
Time's contrails melt to nothing.

Cast

It's almost tomorrow
and there's practically nothing here
except decades-old T-Cut,
the hardener gone off, transmogrified.
Spider husks clench upside down
around a final pain.
All my friends have cleansed the airwaves
of themselves, shrunk
to sightings in Wickes, or
an office cleaning business website
where it's his dad's forearms
modelling frantic dusting.
This time next year
we will be un-extractable.

A buttery sunset
smears down window panes.
Knots in table wood like sepia galaxies.
The need to leave still prickles like static:
too long here would denature you,
corrupt data. Over the wall
next door's apples are golden,
myopia sends them away into myth.
Your life is full of neglected characters.
They shuffle back as stories,
a cast of zombies rounding on you repeatedly
and you know it's one way.

Acknowledgements

Acknowledgements are due to the editors of the following publications and websites where some of these poems first appeared: andotherpoems.wordpress.com, ink-sweat-and-tears.com, *Obsessed with Pipework, Poetry Wales, Magma, Smith's Knoll, Staple, The Poetry Paper, The Rialto, The Rue Bella.*

'In absentia' won joint first prize and 'In Love with Mr Jiggs' third prize respectively, in the 2008 and 2004 Pitshanger Poetry Prizes. An early version of 'Towards Morning' was a Supplementary Prize Winner in the Bridport Poetry Prize. 'Runners-up' was fourth prize winner in the Peterloo Poetry Competition. 'Skinned' was specially commended in the Arvon/Telegraph International Poetry Competition Anthology.

Two short collections, 'The Green Gorilla' and 'The Best Poem Ever Written', included some of the poems printed here and both won first places, in the Biscuit Publishing Poetry Prize 2007 and New Writer Poetry Collection Competition 2006.

'Obvious Constellations', 'On The Dispersal of Water' and 'No Alternative Now' were included in the pamphlet, *Welcome Back to the Country*, published by Seren in 2011, which won the Poetry Wales Purple Moose competition.

Thanks are due to the Poetry Trust, the Jerwood Foundation and, of course, Amy Wack and Seren.